seum of Modern Art, New York

# SIXTEEN AMERICANS

J. DE FEO

WALLY HEDRICK

JAMES JARVAISE

JASPER JOHNS

ELLSWORTH KELLY

ALFRED LESLIE

LANDES LEWITIN

RICHARD LYTLE

ROBERT MALLAR

LOUISE NEVELSO

ROBERT RAUSCHI

JULIUS SCHMIDT

RICHARD STANKI

FRANK STELLA

ALBERT URBAN

JACK YOUNGERM

Distributed by Doubleday & Company, Inc., Garden City, New York

# SIXTEEN AMERICANS

*edited by* DOROTHY C. MILLER *with statements by the artists and others*

THE MUSEUM OF MODERN ART, NEW YORK    1959

Library of Congress Catalog Card Number 59-15966

© The Museum of Modern Art, 1959

11 West 53 Street, New York 19, N.Y.

Printed in the U.S.A. by Connecticut Printers, Inc., Hartford, Connecticut

LENDERS TO THE EXHIBITION

Richard Brown Baker, New York; James Baldwin, Mission, Kansas; Sam Francis,
New York; Walter S. Goodhue, Alexandria, Virginia; Mr. and Mrs. Ira Haupt,
New York; Wally Hedrick, San Francisco; Mr. and Mrs. Ben Heller, New York;
Mr. and Mrs. Richard M. Hollander, Kansas City, Missouri; Rev. Robert C. Hun-
sicker, New York; Jasper Johns, New York; Philip C. Johnson, New York; Mr.
and Mrs. Patrick J. Kelleher, Princeton, New Jersey; Franklin Konigsberg, New
York; J. Patrick Lannan, Chicago; Landès Lewitin, New York; Richard Lytle,
New Haven, Connecticut; Robert Mallary, New York; Royal S. Marks, New
York; Dr. and Mrs. Justin L. Mooney, Mission, Kansas; H. Marc Moyens, Alex-
andria, Virginia; Louise Nevelson, New York; Mr. and Mrs. Albert H. Newman,
Chicago; Mr. and Mrs. Donald H. Peters, New York; Horace Richter, Mt. Gilead,
North Carolina; Mr. and Mrs. William Rubin, New York; Julius Schmidt, Provi-
dence, Rhode Island; Mr. and Mrs. Robert Scull, Great Neck, New York; Mrs.
Albert Urban, New York; Dr. and Mrs. Ernest Zeisler, Chicago.

Leo Castelli Gallery, New York; Dilexi Gallery, San Francisco; Ferus Gallery,
Los Angeles; Rose Fried Gallery, New York; Martha Jackson Gallery, New York;
Felix Landau Gallery, Los Angeles; Betty Parsons Gallery, New York; Stable
Gallery, New York.

Albright Art Gallery, Buffalo, New York.

5

## FOREWORD AND ACKNOWLEDGMENT

*Sixteen Americans,* shown in 1959–60, is another in a series of American group exhibitions which have been presented periodically at the Museum of Modern Art ever since its founding thirty years ago. The work of 140 American artists has been brought before over half a million Museum visitors through these exhibitions, all of which have followed a particular pattern. Preferring not to attempt comprehensive periodic surveys of American art as a whole, a task already undertaken by many other institutions, the Museum devised a different formula for its American group exhibitions: a small number of artists, to be represented by several works each. This pattern may be said to provide, to greater or lesser degree, a series of small one-man shows within the framework of a large exhibition.

Differences rather than similarities in point of view, as well as in age, experience and fame, have been emphasized in these exhibitions at the Museum (the one exception was that held in 1943 devoted to a specific kind of painting—sharp-focus realism). *Sixteen Americans* continues the pattern by bringing together distinct and widely varying personalities, contrasting these personalities sharply rather than attempting to unite them within any given movement or trend. These sixteen are presented simply as individuals and Americans.

Every exhibition has limitations of space which make necessary an arbitary choice of artists. Such a choice is particularly difficult when so few artists are involved but, as in previous exhibitions in the series, the number has been kept low in order to give each artist a separate gallery. And there have been other considerations. The Museum's *Fifteen Americans* in 1952 and *Twelve Americans* in 1956 showed a number of distinguished artists already well known to New York gallery visitors, although far from well known to the Museum's larger public. In the present exhibition it seemed desirable to include a larger proportion of newcomers to the New York scene. Six of the sixteen have not yet had one-man shows in New York and several others have shown but once or have held shows not truly pertinent to their present work. The Museum's recent exhibitions as well as plans for future shows also influenced choices for this one. In any case these choices are not intended as final judgments and are entirely the responsibility of the director of the exhibition who wished to share with the Museum's public some of the interest and excitement experienced in exploring American art in 1959.

Perhaps it is not too much to claim for *Sixteen Americans* an unusually fresh, richly varied, vigorous and youthful character. For those who enjoy statistics, however irrelevant they may be, nine of the sixteen were born in the 1920's, three in the 1930's, and four before 1920. Geographical distribution, not consciously sought after, is nonetheless remarkable: though ten now live in New York City, only one was born here. The other fifteen were born in fourteen different states or countries—California, Connecticut, Egypt, Germany, Indiana, Kentucky, Massachusetts, New Hampshire, New York State, Ohio, Pennsylvania, Russia, South Carolina and Texas. Two now live in San Francisco, one in the Los Angeles area, one in New Haven, one in Providence, Rhode Island.

Whether as a result of years of experiment and achievement or through an early flowering of talent and promise, each artist brings to this exhibition a personal expression distilled out of his own world and thought.

On behalf of the Trustees of the Museum of Modern Art I wish first of all to thank the artists for their participation in the exhibition. I am deeply indebted also to the lenders who have generously made a number of key works of art available. For their contributions to the catalog I am grateful to the artists and to Carl André, E. C. Goossen, Grace Hartigan, Fred Martin, Michael McClure and Robert Rosenblum. Statements were written in 1959 for this catalog unless otherwise noted; the editors of *Arts, Derrière le Miroir,* and *It Is* have graciously permitted quotations from writings published or about to be published in their pages. For special assistance during the preparation of the exhibition my thanks go to Lorser Feitelson and Jack Von Dornum of Los Angeles, Walter S. Goodhue of Alexandria, Virginia, Ted Haseltine of New York, Richard Hollander and George L. McKenna of Kansas City, Sam Hunter of Minneapolis, Fred Martin and the Art Bank of the San Francisco Art Association, and Gordon M. Smith of Buffalo. Photographs of the artists were taken by Joseph Breitenbach, Donald Cook, J. De Feo, Sante Forlano, Hollis Frampton, Kay Harris, Wally Hedrick, Jeremiah Russell, Delmore Scott, Walt Silver, Hall Winslow; works of art were photographed by Oliver Baker, Rudolph Burckhardt, Paul Cordes, Irwin Gooen, Robert Mallary, William Maund, Edward Meneeley, Kay Neer, Julius Schmidt, Richard Stankiewicz, Soichi Sunami.

Dorothy C. Miller
*Director of the Exhibition*

photograph Wally Hedrick

## J. DE FEO

Only by chancing the ridiculous, can I hope for the sublime. Only by discovering that which is true within myself, can I hope to be understood by others.

I regard myself as an expressionist as well as a symbolist. If expressionism implies emotional impact, I can realize it only by restraint and ultimate refinement.

—J. DE FEO

*For Jay De Feo:* Many themes have been re-current, and world-things have had names for you and you have said them: Rose, jewel, avalanche on Everest, jazz and womb. They have been announced to you both in the after-time and before because they roll round you, are timeless to your star and fodder for its eternity. In this way you have been fed by much; all things, beating onward have called on you for dwelling. Surely in you a place would be opened for their destiny.

And you made a space of wings whence your soul might look out, as in its forehead began the star. All this, that for you and for us there be radiance.

—FRED MARTIN

". . . not her love for you, but the gesture of her feelings. Love, anguish, labor, confrontations of herself with herself. Not my sight or your sight but hers!"

—MICHAEL MC CLURE

8

J. De Feo: *Deathrose*. Unfinished oil painting begun in 1958. *Not in the exhibition*

10

e: J. De Feo: *Origin*. 1956. Oil, 7′8¼″ x 6′7¾″. Dilexi Gallery

J. De Feo: *The Veronica*. 1957. Oil, 11′ x 42½″. Ferus Gallery

J. De Feo: *Death Wish*. 1958. Charcoal, graphite, oil on paper, 7' x 43". Collection J. Patrick Lannan

J. De Feo: *Daphne*. 1958. Charcoal, graphite, oil on paper, 8'10" x 41½". Collection Sam Francis

12

# WALLY HEDRICK

I have tried to arrange things so that I can do what I want.

No one ever likes the painting that I'm working on.

I like this because this means that the things I'm thinking about in my head are still mine (i.e., no one has ever thought of them before).

Modern art is very popular nowadays—almost every one can do it and does. Painting has changed but people have not—they do what they have to, they do what they can do or what they have learned to do. This is my definition of the student painter: a man walks up to another and asks "man, how do you do it?" The one asked is tired, the asker will never get sleepy.

Whenever I do something I try to do it the best way I can. I like a woman after I've made love to her because I know her. I like my paintings after I've painted them because I knew it was a good idea or I wouldn't have bothered. One day you wake up and painting isn't mental gymnastics, it is not done to get a grade, it is not done to get in shows nor is it done to stop thinking. IT'S JUST DONE!

When I paint I must take nothing and make something—so one has to accept the technical problems as such but the main ingredient that is needed is an IDEA.

He who has an idea cannot be stopped except by himself. I understand that lots of people don't have ideas and can't find them in the yellow section. If you can grab the spirit of the idea with your technique and have enough time you

13

Wally Hedrick: *Spirit, 3.* 1958. Oil, 69¾ x 52¾". Owned by the artist

Wally Hedrick: *Around Painting*. 1957. Oil, 69¾" diameter. Owned by the artist

Wally Hedrick: *Circle Painting, 4.* 1957. Oil, 65¾ x 58". Owned by the artist

Wally Hedrick: *For Service Rendered.* 1959.
Oil, 40¾ x 35". Owned by the artist

16

Hedrick: *Heroic Image*. 1959.
x 71". Owned by the artist

can come up with something. For me these things or "somethings" have no particular stylistic continuity—they can or not, I don't care.

I sometimes draw upon ways of working employed when I was younger, other
times I have to develop new ways of putting over the IDEA, again I must make it
clear that all this talk about technique and what people do or don't do is really
incidental to the product. There are many poets in this world but few bother to
write poems.

I hope that people will look at my things as individuals. I hope that my things
will stand alone. I am right behind them. —WALLY HEDRICK

17

photograph Delmore Scott

## JAMES JARVAISE

For the past two years I have been painting a series of landscapes. At the outset, I did not see that the early paintings in this series were landscapes. Gradually, however, I became aware that these paintings reflected the world that surrounded my home. To date these paintings, which I call the Hudson River School Series, fall into two distinct groups. In the first group—all on masonite, completed in 1957–58—large white areas tend to dominate the painting. In the second group—all on canvas, completed in 1958–59—a gradual change occurs, with increasingly subtle colors becoming dominant and the white areas diminishing or even disappearing.

In the process of translating my reactions to my surroundings, I have acquired a new understanding of previous generations of American landscape painters. I have come to feel a special sympathy for such artists as Thomas Cole, Asher B. Durand, John Kensett, and Frederick Church. It is to these Hudson River School painters that I have dedicated my own landscapes. —JAMES JARVAISE

18

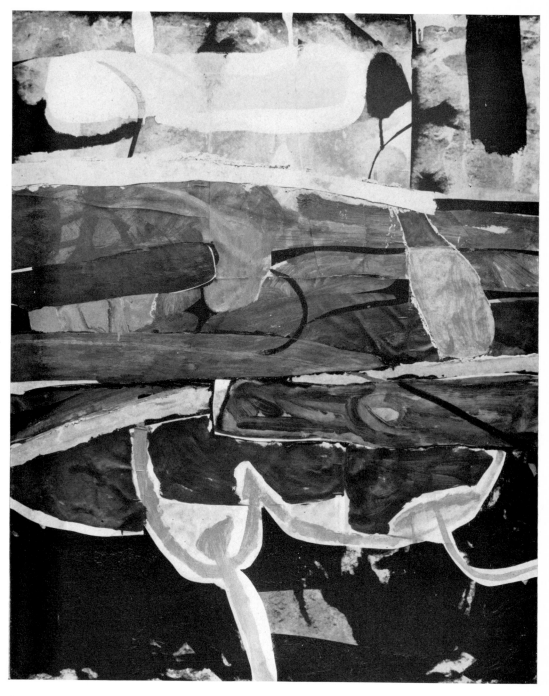

James Jarvaise: *Hudson River School Series, 59.* 1958. Collage and oil, 60 x 48″. Felix Landau
Gallery

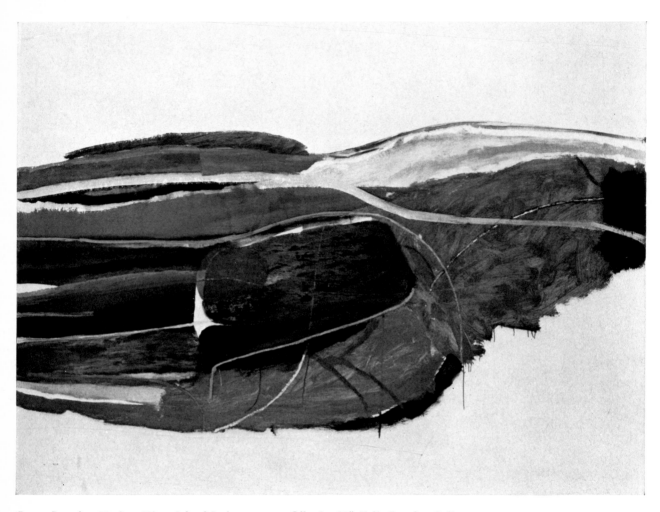

James Jarvaise: *Hudson River School Series, 30.* 1957. Oil, 48 x 66". Felix Landau Gallery

opposite: James Jarvaise: *Hudson River School Series, 8*
Oil, 60 x 55½". Felix Landau Gallery

## JASPER JOHNS

Sometimes I see it and then paint it. Other times I paint it and then see it. Both are impure situations, and I prefer neither.

At every point in nature there is something to see. My work contains similar possibilities for the changing focus of the eye.

Three academic ideas which have been of interest to me are what a teacher of mine (speaking of Cézanne and cubism) called "the rotating point of view" (Larry Rivers recently pointed to a black rectangle, two or three feet away from where he had been looking in a painting, and said ". . . like there's something happening over there too."); Marcel Duchamp's suggestion "to reach the Impossibility of sufficient visual memory to transfer from one like object to another the memory imprint"; and Leonardo's idea ("Therefore, O painter, do not surround your bodies with lines . . .") that the boundary of a body is neither a part of the enclosed body nor a part of the surrounding atmosphere.

Generally, I am opposed to painting which is concerned with conceptions of simplicity. Everything looks very busy to me. —JASPER JOHNS

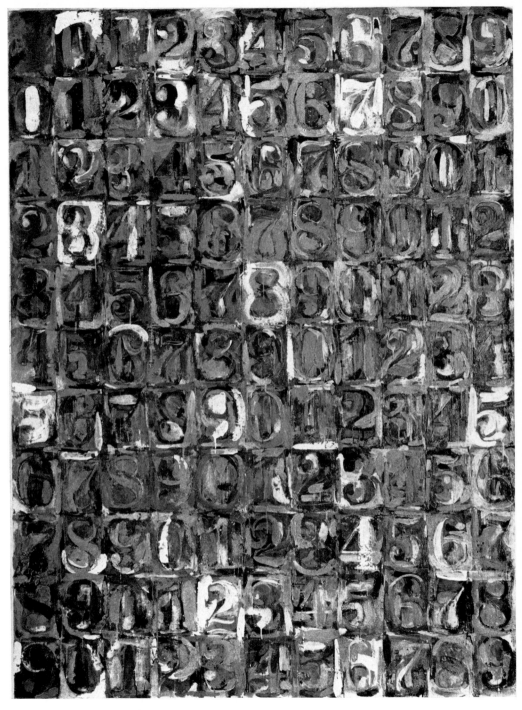

Jasper Johns: *Numbers in Color*. 1958–59. Encaustic on newspaper, 67 x 49½". Albright Art Gallery, Buffalo, New York. Gift of Seymour H. Knox

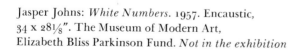

Jasper Johns: *Tennyson*. 1958. Encaustic on newspaper, 73½ x 48¼". Collection Mr. and Mrs. Donald
H. Peters

Jasper Johns: *White Numbers*. 1957. Encaustic,
34 x 28⅛". The Museum of Modern Art,
Elizabeth Bliss Parkinson Fund. *Not in the exhibition*

þer Johns: *Large White Flag*. 1955. Encaustic on newspaper, 12′ x 6′. Owned by the artist

Jasper Johns: *Black Target*. 1959. Encaustic on newspaper, 54 x 54″. Leo Castelli Gallery

Jasper Johns: *Target with Four Faces*. 1955. Encaustic on newspaper, 26 x 26″. The Museum of Modern Art

Jasper Johns: *Green Target*. 1955. Encaustic and collage, 60 x 60". The Museum of Modern Art, Richard S. Zeisler Fund

**ELLSWORTH KELLY**

photograph Sante Forlano

That there is something more to be said through brilliance, clarity and subtlety is apparent upon one's first intimate contact with the art of Ellsworth Kelly. But this very clarity and brilliance is apt to startle one into confusion by its immediacy. In his boldness he fires directly through the whole encampment of the plastic arts, past the sentries whose special orders are to prevent infiltration from one service area to the next, and past the gate-keepers (poor souls) who are forever trying to keep the barrels of their categories clean. Kelly follows where his instinct leads him . . .

One of the first things one notes in Kelly's best pictures is the unity of surface. Despite the rectangle, expressed in distinctly differentiated colors, there is none of that nerve-wracking oscillation or that electronic "jump" one encounters in much painting today . . .

Kelly's work, while neither so idealistic nor as stripped down as Mondrian's, is, on the contemporary scene, a calming, slightly ironic statement and a cooling corrective.

. . . Mondrian certainly thought of and wanted to use his intersecting blacks as vital and morally expressive (though not quite as sensuous). And Barnett Newman, through the masterly development of his surfaces has found maximum

Ellsworth Kelly: *Falcon*. 1959. Oil, 60 x 49". Betty Parsons Gallery

Ellsworth Kelly: *Slip*. 1959. Oil,
60 x 50". Betty Parsons Gallery

opposite: Ellsworth Kelly: *Wave*
1959. Oil, 60" x 7'10". Betty Parso

sensuousness within the rectangle of his color field. With Kelly the color lies on the surface (it is a kind of spaceless skin) and though it plays an important role in the sensuous result, the true burden of the sensuous excitement is carried by the contours. The hard, crisp edges command the eye to feel them as the hand would feel soft flesh. The emotion is like that we sustain before sculpture.

—E. C. GOOSSEN

From *Derrière le Miroir,* No. 110, Editions Pierre à Feu, A. Maeght, Editor, Paris, 1958.

Ellsworth Kelly: *York*. 1959. Oil, 68 x 88". Betty Parsons Gallery

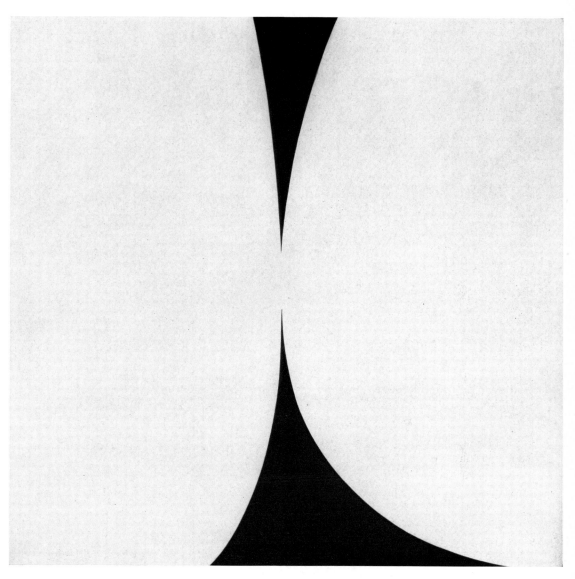

Ellsworth Kelly: *Rebound*. 1959. Oil, 68¼ x 71½". Collection Franklin Konigsberg

photograph Walt Silver

## ALFRED LESLIE

It seems to me that lately all my conversations have been about fear. I think that courage is admirable, but to be brave one must know what it is to be afraid—anything else is bravura.

Alfred Leslie's paintings are strong because he knows how to be weak. They are beautiful because they triumph over ugliness. In all of Leslie's work his gentleness pursues his power relentlessly and unforgivingly.

We see the golden chain, the velvet glove, the rose and thorn, the green that in the city will satisfy forever the hunger for trees and grass, and because it is city green it is larger than life—monster green.

In the expression of my generation, which turns to irony on one hand and rhetoric on the other, it is infinitely moving to come upon true and controlled passion. —GRACE HARTIGAN

34

fred Leslie: *Baby's Curse*. 1959. Oil, 6′ x 7′. Martha Jackson Gallery

Alfred Leslie: *The Second Two-panel Horizontal.* 1958. Oil, 6' x 11'. Martha Jackson Gallery

Alfred Leslie: *The Four-panel Green.* 1957. Oil, 12' x 11'4". Martha Jackson

Landès Lewitin: *Forget It.* c.1954. Oil, 21 x 34″. Rose Fried Gallery

## LANDÈS LEWITIN

An enchantment celestialized, a secret content, flexible to the evolution of the thought, meeting the eyes, caracoling, grasping the mind, leaving memory halos of hue saturations, or lightly hued supplications with dove-whiteness.

Sometimes a hard fluidity of a staring muteness, exclusive and latent, evoking festive days. Then again the starkness of megaliths, dolmen, cromlechs and menhirs. —LANDÈS LEWITIN

To be published in a forthcoming issue of *It Is.*

Landès Lewitin: *Knockout*. 1955–59. Oil and glass, 23⅞ x 17⅞". Rose Fried Gallery

Landès Lewitin: *And They Never Change*. 1957–58. Plastic emulsion, 40 x 60". Collection Royal S. Marks

Landès Lewitin: *Think of Me, Dear.* c.1956. Oil and plastic, 23 x 11″. Rose Fried Gallery

Landès Lewitin: *Easy.* 1955–58. Oil and plastic, 34 x 21″. Collection Royal S. Marks

**RICHARD LYTLE**

Within the process of painting universes wait unexplored. The quest for these worlds has led painters to seek plastic relationships which transcend the historical concept of subject matter and which glorify the possibilities of color. To embrace human experience with a complexity of space and color logical within its own bounds and yet not without focus is the adventure. Delacroix wrote in his diary: "In many people the eye is untrue or inert; they see the objects literally; of the exquisite they see nothing." The challenge is to inflame strong images that can evoke deep emotional and intellectual responses united with those responses felt by human beings concerned with the relationships of man to nature and of man to man. —RICHARD LYTLE

Richard Lytle: *The Possessed*. 1959. Oil, 8'2″ x 6'7″. Owned by the artist

44

Richard Lytle: *Icarus Descended*. 1958. Oil, 62⅜ x 70¼″. The Museum of Modern Art, Elizabeth Bliss Parkinson Fund

e: Richard Lytle: *Prometheus*. 1959. Oil, 6′7″ x 71″. Owned by the artist

45

Richard Lytle: *Verge*. 1959. Oil, 71″ x 6′7″. Owned by the artist

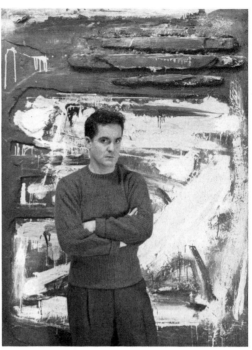

photograph Donald Cook

# ROBERT MALLARY

I conceive of an image as a monolith, an actual object in an actual place, aggressive in the factuality of its physical and sculptural attributes of surface, shape and substance. But it is an object which is magically dissolving and forming and in a state of tension with its pictorial attributes of seeming, intimating and conjuring. The irregularities of its surface and outer shape emphasize its sculpturality but also are a response to the pictorial forces set loose within it. The protrusions and recessions establish "framed" areas within the monolith, isolating, enclosing and also linking "movements," "chapters," "acts," "scenes" and "stanzas." In this situation the impasto of painting sometimes preserves its pictorial "skin" and at other times is transformed into sculpture.

In other words I am intrigued with that bastard area where the painted and sculptured object is uncertain of its parentage.

If my arm is twisted and I have to choose sides—well, then I'm more a painter than a sculptor.

I like the absence of colors. I also like those colors that are usually called tones —browns, greys, umbers and siennas. Also bright colors—but these mainly on weekends.

If artists are not ideologists they are opportunists who look ahead, or up or

Robert Mallary: *Prison Yard*. 1959. Composition stone in resin base, 6'9½" x 57¾".
Owned by the artist

bert Mallary: *In Flight.* 1957. Wood, polyester resin, paint, sand on plywood, 43½″ x 6′7⅝″. The Museum of Modern Art

backwards, or to the right or the left. These days I mainly look down. And I see rivers and skies around my feet, vast spaces transfixed in inches of concrete.

The accidental in art can serve as a metaphor for nature. The problem is to grasp the inevitable in the accident and make it art. In other words, art and nature in stress within the single work. —ROBERT MALLARY

49

Robert Mallary: *Head of Bull*. 1958. Composition stone in resin base, 33 x 33″. Owned by the artist

Robert Mallary: *Nambe*. 1958. Compositi◁
resin base, 6′5″ x 49″. Collection Philip C.◁

50

photograph Jeremiah Russell

# LOUISE NEVELSON

In some ways, Louise Nevelson's newest and most astonishing achievements—her vast wooden walls—recall the iconoclastic innovations of the new American painting . . . which similarly impose upon the spectator an engulfing sensuous environment . . .

. . . Traditionally, the fragile, private quality of Nevelson's imagination implies (and here one thinks of Klee) an equally intimate scale; and to see this personal world magnified to public dimensions is a startling experience for which perhaps only the architectural fantasies of Gaudi or the largest Abstract Expressionist paintings offer adequate preparation . . . Yet even after one has assimilated the disarming scale of this imagination, further heresies remain. An unfamiliar lack of permanence and aesthetic inevitability is intended here, for not only are these physically separate but visually fused boxes capable of infinite rearrangement, but even their number might be diminished or increased. Moreover, the fantastically varied excrescences of this architectural framework—splats, moldings, a carved leaf—appear to be growing slowly but irrevocably, like stalactites in a darkened grotto, and underline the sense that the whole exists in an animate state, almost transforming itself as we observe it. Is there perhaps here a surprising translation of those qualities of chance so prominent in today's painting

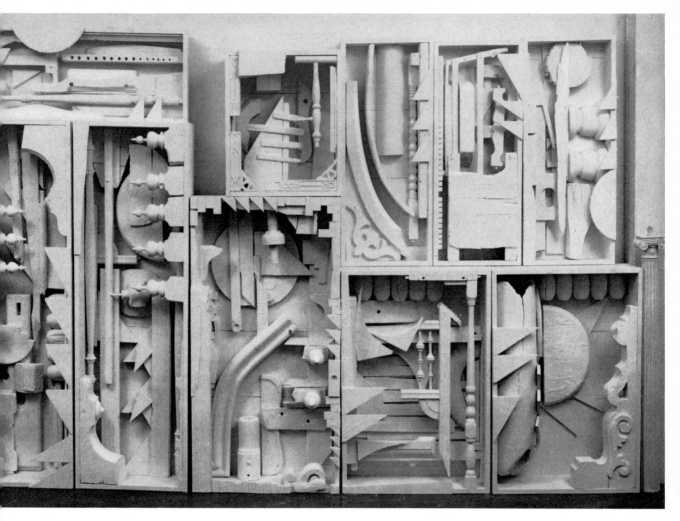

Nevelson: *Dawn's Wedding Feast* (one section). 1959. Wood wall construction, painted white, about 16′ wide. Martha Jackson ... Photograph Rudolph Burckhardt

into the less accident-prone realm of constructed sculpture? Yet in Nevelson's art, as in that of the best painters who work with a vocabulary of constant flux, each seemingly random configuration is guided by an experienced intuition which stamps both the parts and the whole with the quality of a distinctive and controlled style. And like the best of recent painting, too, Nevelson's work has the authority to compel the spectator to re-examine his prejudices—as well as the sensuous and imaginative richness to repay this effort. —ROBERT ROSENBLUM

From "Louise Nevelson" in *Arts Yearbook 3: Paris/New York,* 1959.

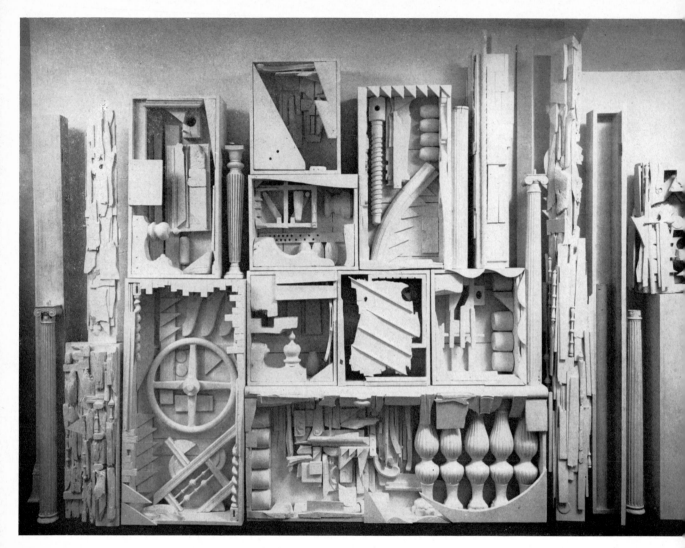

Louise Nevelson: *Dawn's Wedding Feast* (one section). 1959. Wood wall construction, painted white, about 16' wide. Martha Jackson Gallery. Detail opposite. Photograph Rudolph Burckhardt

Louise Nevelson: *Dawn's Wedding Feast* (detail). 1959. Wood constructions, painted white.
Martha Jackson Gallery. Photograph Rudolph Burckhardt

right: Louise Nevelson: *Sky Cathedral*. 1958. Wood wall construction, painted black, 11'3½" high
The Museum of Modern Art, gift of Mr. and Mrs. Ben Mildwoff. Photograph Soichi Sunami.
*Not in the exhibition but on view elsewhere in the Museum*

photograph Kay Harris

## ROBERT RAUSCHENBERG

Any incentive to paint is as good as any other. There is no poor subject.

Painting is always strongest when in spite of composition, color, etc. it appears as a fact, or an inevitability, as opposed to a souvenir or arrangement.

Painting relates to both art and life. Neither can be made. (I try to act in that gap between the two.)

A pair of socks is no less suitable to make a painting with than wood, nails, turpentine, oil and fabric.

A canvas is never empty. —ROBERT RAUSCHENBERG

58

Robert Rauschenberg: *Summer Storm*. 1959. Combine-painting, 6'7" x 63". Collection Mr. and Mrs. Ira Haupt

Robert Rauschenberg: *Satellite*. 1955. Combine-painting with pheasant, 6'8" x 42½". Collection Dr. and Mrs. Ernest Zeisler

Robert Rauschenberg: *Curfew*. 1958. Combine-painting, 57¼ x 39½". Collection Mr. and Mrs. Donald H. Peters

Robert Rauschenberg: *The Magician*. 1959. Combine-painting, 65½ x 38½".
Collection Mrs. Leo Castelli

**JULIUS SCHMIDT**

From the machine form comes a powerful stimulation and expression. A stimulation is derived from its reminiscence of plants, animals and the natural processes. An expression of contained life, growth, energy and order seems also to carry the image of man's power, of his usefulness and his uselessness.

How can an image of contemporary civilized-uncivilized man be possible without that form which he has pursued these thousands of years?

The sculpture is carved in reverse in blocks of core sand, a fine sand mixed with a binder which when baked becomes a permeable but hard block, easy to carve but strong enough to withstand the heat and pressure of molten metal. The carving is done with various abrasive tools. From the carved blocks a multiple piece mold is assembled, its cavities fitted with various cores to make the sculpture hollow and with sprues, runners and gates to allow the metal to flow to every part. Now the molten metal is poured into the finished mold. When cool, the mold is smashed off and the sculpture emerges. —JULIUS SCHMIDT

Julius Schmidt: *Iron sculpture.* 1958. Cast iron, 68″ high. William Rockhill Nelson Gallery of Art and Atkins Museum of Fine Arts, Kansas City, gift of Mr. and Mrs. Herman R. Sutherland, Mr. William T. Kemper, and the Mid-American Annual Purchase Fund. *Not in the exhibition*

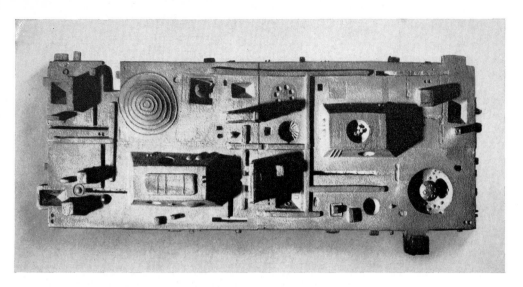

Julius Schmidt: *Iron sculpture.* 1958. Cast iron relief, 14 x 31″. Owned by the artist

Julius Schmidt: *Bronze sculpture.* 1958. Cast bronze, 23″ long. Collection Walter S. Goodhue

s Schmidt: *Iron sculpture*. 1959. Cast
copper plated, 6' high. Owned by the
Photograph Kay Neer

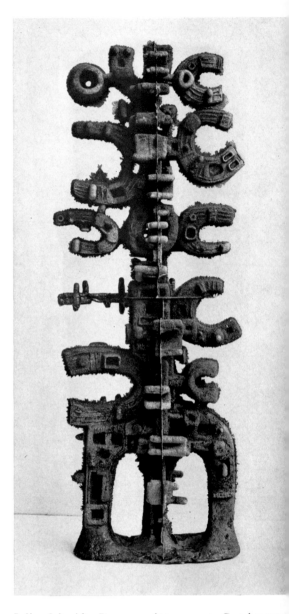

Julius Schmidt: *Bronze sculpture*. 1958. Cast bronze, 24″ high. Collection Mr. and Mrs. Patrick J. Kelleher

Julius Schmidt: *Bronze sculpture*. 1957. Cast bronze, 23″ high. Collection James Baldwin

68

Julius Schmidt: *Iron sculpture*. 1958. Cast iron, 13″ long. Collection Rev. Robert C. Hunsicker

Studio showing core sand molds, tools, working drawings and small sculptures

photograph Walt Silver

# RICHARD STANKIEWICZ

Things may be objectively present without having the affective power that we call "presence." The extraordinary object, the one with presence, is one which is subjectively and tyrannically there: it can no more be ignored than being stared at can. It seems to me that this charged quality of things is what a work must have to be sculpture and any technical means for achieving it is allowable. It is the ultimate realism, this presence, having nothing to do with resemblances to "nature." The peculiar posture of the convincing being, the stance of being about to move, the enormity of the immovable, the tension between the separate parts of a whole are qualities that pull us to the special object like iron to a magnet. And these beings of presence that we try to make—they are models of a never quite credible existence. —RICHARD STANKIEWICZ

Richard Stankiewicz: *Committee*. 1954.
Steel, 14″ high. Collection Horace Richter

Richard Stankiewicz: *Urchin in the Grass*. 1956. Iron
and steel, 23½″ high. Collection Philip C. Johnson

71

Richard Stankiewicz: *Fish Lurking*. 1958. Iron and steel, 48¼″ high. Collection Mr. and Mrs. Albert H. Newman

Richard Stankiewicz: *Travels of the Pussycat King.*
1957. Iron and steel, 13″ high. Collection Richard
Brown Baker

chard Stankiewicz: *Instruction.* 1957. Iron and steel, 12½″
h. The Museum of Modern Art, Philip C. Johnson Fund.
otograph Soichi Sunami

Richard Stankiewicz: *Panel*. 1955. Iron and steel 68″ x 11′9″. Stable Gallery. Photograph Soichi Sunami

opposite: Richard Stankiewicz: *Diving to the Bottom of the* 1958. Iron and steel, 54½″ high. Private collection

photograph Hollis Frampton

**FRANK STELLA**

Preface to Stripe Painting
Art excludes the unnecessary. Frank Stella has found it necessary to paint stripes. There is nothing else in his painting.

Frank Stella is not interested in expression or sensitivity. He is interested in the necessities of painting.

Symbols are counters passed among people. Frank Stella's painting is not symbolic. His stripes are the paths of brush on canvas. These paths lead only into painting. —CARL ANDRÉ

76

ella: *Die Fahne Hoch!* 1959. Oil,
 6'. Leo Castelli Gallery

Frank Stella: *Tomlinson Cou*
1959. Oil, 7'1" x 9'1¾". Leo
Gallery

Frank Stella: *The Marriage of*
*and Squalor.* 1959. Oil, 7'6¾" x
Leo Castelli Gallery

Stella: *Arundel Castle*. 1959. Oil,
⅔" x 6'1". Leo Castelli Gallery

**ALBERT URBAN**

photograph Joseph Breitenbach

Like so much of the best recent American painting, Albert Urban's last works distill from art and from nature an elemental, irreducible experience. From art, they choose the most single-minded vocabulary—one glowing hue, one primary shape; from nature, the most basic forces—heat, light, energy. In this, their majestic breadth and indivisibility evoke ultimates. Before these incandescent orbits, one thinks of the poetry of Genesis, of the flaming birth and freezing death of planets, stars, the universe.

Yet once more, as with the finest art of the 1950's, these presumably primitive statements are achieved with a pictorial sophistication that contradicts any facile description of Urban's canvases as being composed of circular movements and single or few hues. For example, their radiant color, even when limited to a solitary green or yellow, surpasses the nuance and sensuousness of many more superficially abundant palettes; and when two colors are used—a blue or a cerise against a burning orange—their acid collision extracts a pictorial drama of rare power from such ostensibly simple techniques. Similarly, the very substance of this art belies definition, for its molten, gyrating forces hover in a changing balance between solid and void, between coalescence and dissolution. Moreover, the apparent circularity of these works is far less predictable than it may at first

80

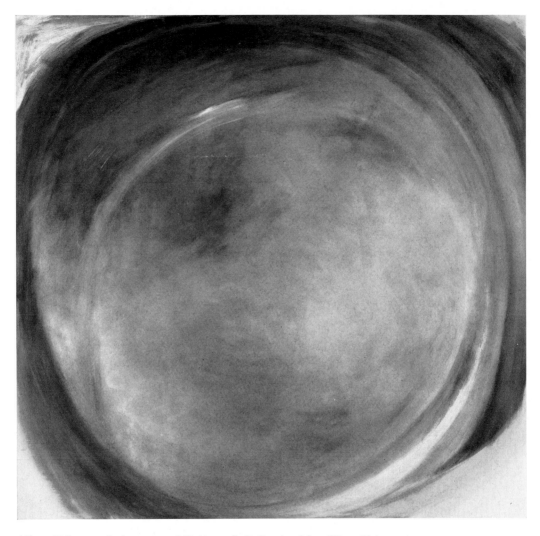

Albert Urban: *Painting*. 1959. Oil, 68 x 70". Collection Mrs. Albert Urban

seem, complicated as it is by unexpected magnetisms. Suddenly, a minor external element will exert a major gravitational pull; or a concealed, off-center focus will establish a compelling, contrapuntal polarity.

Like the cosmic imagery it parallels, Urban's art absorbs the spectator by deriving order from primeval chaos, diversity from awesome oneness. As such, it again reminds us that in the last decade the richest rewards for the eye and the imagination have most often been attained through the simplest pictorial means.

—ROBERT ROSENBLUM

81

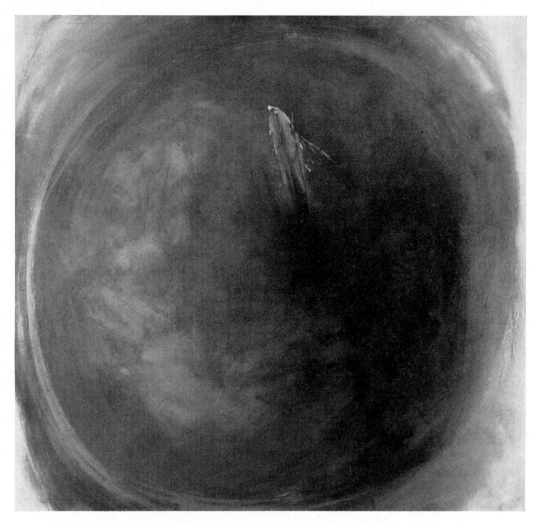

Albert Urban: *Painting*. 1959. Oil, 54 x 56". Collection Mrs. Albert Urban

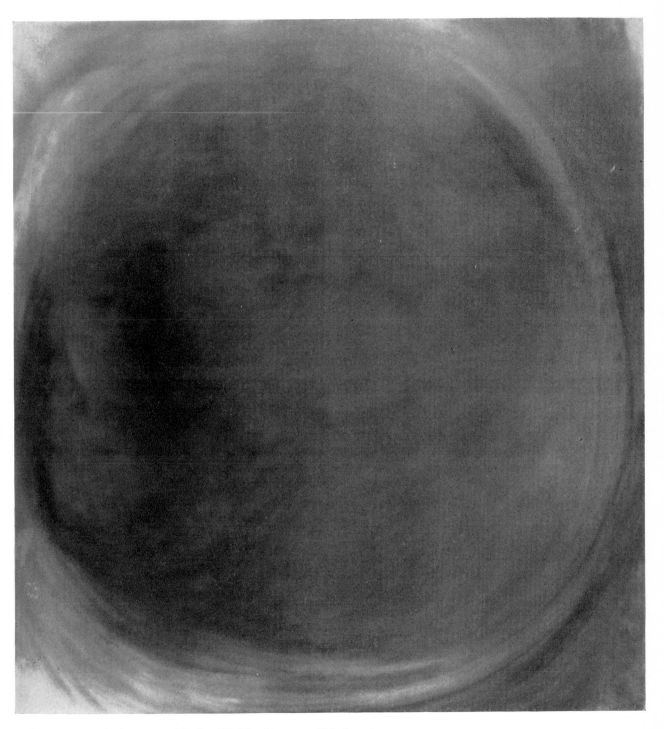

Albert Urban: *Painting*. 1959. Oil, 6′ x 68″. The Museum of Modern Art

photograph Hall Winslow

**JACK YOUNGERMAN**

Jack Youngerman: *Aquitaine*. 1959. Oil, 70 x 49½". The Museum of Modern Art, Larry Aldrich Foundation Fund

Jack Youngerman: *Ram*. 1959. Oil, 7′6″ x 63½″. Betty Parsons Gallery

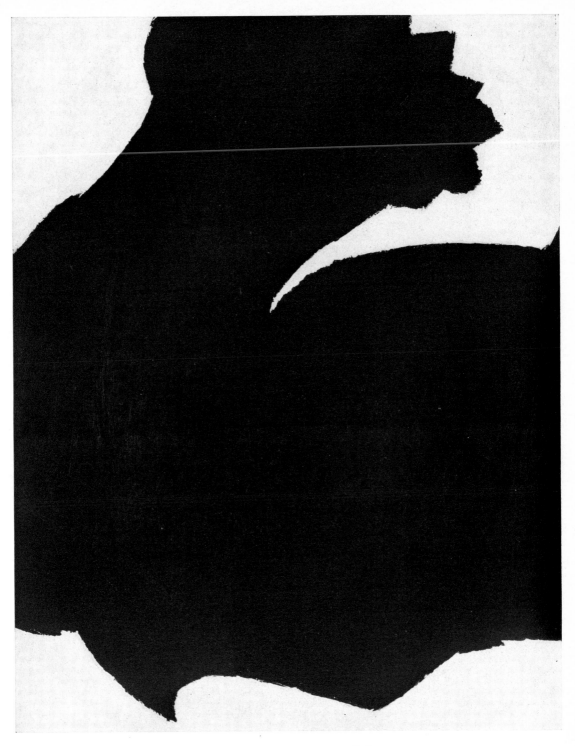

Jack Youngerman: *Big Black*. 1959. Oil, 7'7" x 70". Betty Parsons Gallery

Jack Youngerman: *Aztec III*. 1959. Oil, 6′3″ x 7′1″. Private collection

Jack Youngerman: *Coenties Slip.* 1959. Oil, 6'9" x 63". Betty Parsons Gallery

BIOGRAPHIES OF THE ARTISTS AND LIST OF WORKS OF ART

*An asterisk preceding the title indicates that the work is illustrated. In the dimensions of the paintings, height precedes width. Lenders to the exhibition are listed on page 5.*

## J. DE FEO

Born in Hanover, New Hampshire, March 31, 1929. To California about 1931; has lived in and around San Francisco ever since. University of California, Berkeley, 1946–51; B.A. and M.A. degrees. Won Sigmund Martin Heller Traveling Fellowship, 1951; in Europe, chiefly in Florence, Italy, 1951–53. In many group exhibitions in California since 1950. One-man show: Dilexi Gallery, San Francisco, 1959.

*Origin.* 1956. Oil on canvas, 7′8¼″ x 6′7¾″. Lent by Dilexi Gallery, San Francisco. Ill. p. 10

*The Veronica.* 1957. Oil on canvas, 11′ x 42½″. Lent by Ferus Gallery, Los Angeles. Ill. p. 11

*Persephone.* 1957. Graphite on paper mounted on canvas, 7′8½″ x 41½″. Lent by J. Patrick Lannan, Chicago

*Daphne.* 1958. Charcoal, graphite, oil on paper mounted on canvas, 8′10″ x 41½″. Lent by Sam Francis, New York. Ill. p. 12

*Death Wish.* 1958. Charcoal, graphite, oil on paper mounted on canvas 7′ x 43″. Lent by J. Patrick Lannan, Chicago. Ill. p. 12

## WALLY HEDRICK

Born in Pasadena, California, 1928. Studied at Otis Art Institute, Los Angeles; College of Arts and Crafts, Oakland, California; California School of Fine Arts, San Francisco, B.F.A. degree; San Francisco State College, M.F.A. degree. Teaches at California School of Fine Arts. Lives in San Francisco. Has exhibited in group shows since 1953. One-man shows: Area Arts, San Francisco,

1954; M. H. De Young Memorial Museum, San Francisco, 1955; San Francisco Art Association Gallery, 1956; Oakland Art Museum, 1958. In collections of Oakland Art Museum and Los Angeles County Museum.

*Around Painting.* 1957. Oil on canvas, 69¾″ diameter. Lent by the artist. Ill. p. 15

*Circle Painting, 4.* 1957. Oil on canvas, 65¾ x 58″. Lent by the artist. Ill. p. 16

*Circle Painting, 6.* 1957. Oil on canvas, 59¾″ diameter. Lent by the artist

*Spirit Plus Idea, 1.* 1958. Oil on canvas, 40 x 30″. Lent by the artist

*The Spirit.* 1958. Oil on canvas, 38 x 35¾″. Lent by the artist

*Spirit, 3.* 1958. Oil on canvas, 69¾ x 52¾″. Lent by the artist. Ill. p. 14

*Spirit Plus Idea, 12.* 1958. Oil on canvas, 65½ x 58″. Lent by the artist

*Heroic Image.* 1959. Oil on canvas, hexagonal, 61 x 71″. Lent by the artist. Ill. p. 17

*For Service Rendered.* 1959. Oil on canvas, 40¾ x 35″. Lent by the artist. Ill. p. 16

## JAMES JARVAISE

Born in Indianapolis, Indiana, February 16, 1925. Lived in Pittsburgh from about 1930 to 1940; then to Los Angeles. Studied painting during grade school with Sam Rosenberg at Carnegie Institute; later studied with James Fitzpatrick. In U.S. Army Air Force, 1943–45. In 1945 studied briefly at a small art school in Biarritz. Attended University of Southern California, 1947–52; B.F.A. and M.F.A. degrees. In Europe, 1953–55, spending much time in southern France. Has taught since 1955 at University of Southern California. Lives in Altadena, California. In group exhibitions since 1952, including Carnegie International, Pittsburgh, 1958. One-man shows: Felix Landau Gallery, Los Angeles, 1952, 1955, 1958. In collections of Addison Gallery of American Art, Andover,

Massachusetts; Los Angeles County Museum; Carnegie Institute, Pittsburgh; Butler Art Institute, Youngstown, Ohio.

*Hudson River School Series, 30.* 1957. Oil on masonite, 48 x 66". Lent by Felix Landau Gallery, Los Angeles. Ill. p. 20

*Hudson River School Series, 50.* 1958. Oil on canvas, 51 x 45". Lent by Felix Landau Gallery, Los Angeles

*Hudson River School Series, 59.* 1958. Collage and oil on gesso panel, 60 x 48". Lent by Felix Landau Gallery, Los Angeles. Ill. p. 19

*Hudson River School Series, L2.* 1959. Oil on canvas, 6'11½" x 67". Lent by Felix Landau Gallery, Los Angeles

*Hudson River School Series, 86.* 1959. Oil on canvas, 60 x 55½". Lent by Felix Landau Gallery, Los Angeles. Ill. p. 21

*Hudson River School Series, 87.* 1959. Oil on canvas, 66 x 55¼". Lent by Felix Landau Gallery, Los Angeles

## JASPER JOHNS

Born in Allendale, South Carolina, May 15, 1930. At University of South Carolina, Columbia, two years. In U.S. Army two years; six months in Japan. Has lived in New York since 1952. One-man shows: Leo Castelli, 1958; Galerie Rive Droite, Paris, 1959; Galleria d'Arte del Naviglio, Milan, 1959. In various group shows since 1956, including international exhibitions: Carnegie International, Pittsburgh, 1958; one of three Americans in exhibition of young Italian and foreign artists, 29th Biennale, Venice, 1958; Exposition Internationale du Surréalisme, Paris, 1959–60. In collections of Albright Art Gallery, Buffalo, New York; Museum of Modern Art, New York.

*Large Flag.* 1954. Encaustic on newspaper on canvas, 42 x 60". Lent by Philip C. Johnson, New York

*Green Target.* 1955. Encaustic on newspaper on canvas, 60 x 60". The Museum of Modern Art, New York, Richard S. Zeisler Fund. Ill. p. 27

*Large White Flag.* 1955. Encaustic on newspaper on canvas, 12' x 6' in 3 sections. Lent by the artist. Ill. p. 25

*Grey Alphabets.* 1956. Encaustic on newspaper on canvas, 66 x 46". Lent by Mr. and Mrs. Ben Heller, New York

*Large White Numbers.* 1958. Encaustic on canvas, 67 x 49½". Lent by Mr. and Mrs. Robert Scull, Great Neck, New York

*Tennyson.* 1958. Encaustic on newspaper on canvas, 6'11½" x 48¼". Lent by Mr. and Mrs. Donald H. Peters, New York. Ill. p. 24

*White Target.* 1958. Encaustic on newspaper on canvas, 42¾ x 42½". Lent by Leo Castelli Gallery, New York

*Numbers in Color.* 1958–59. Encaustic on newspaper on canvas, 67 x 49½". Lent by Albright Art Gallery, Buffalo, New York, Gift of Seymour H. Knox. Ill. p. 23

*Black Target.* 1959. Encaustic on newspaper on canvas, 54 x 54". Lent by Leo Castelli Gallery, New York. Ill. p. 26

## ELLSWORTH KELLY

Born in Newburgh, New York, May 31, 1923. Studied at School of the Museum of Fine Arts, Boston, and Ecole des Beaux-Arts, Paris. In U.S. Army Engineers Corps, 1943–46. Lived in Paris, 1948–54; in New York since 1954. Commissions: large painted metal relief for Transportation Building, Philadelphia, 1956–57; plastic mosaic mural for Eastmore House, New York. One-man shows: Galerie Arnaud, Paris, 1951; Betty Parsons Gallery, New York, 1956, 1957, 1959; Galerie Maeght, Paris, 1958. In various group exhibitions in Europe and America, including Seventeen Contemporary American Painters, United States Pavilion, Brussels World's Fair, 1958. In collections of Albright Art Gallery, Buffalo, New York; Whitney Museum of American Art, New York; Carnegie Institute, Pittsburgh.

*Charter.* 1959. Oil on canvas, 7'6" x 60". Lent by Betty Parsons Gallery, New York

*Falcon.* 1959. Oil on canvas, 60 x 49". Lent by Betty Parsons Gallery, New York. Ill. p. 29

*Rebound.* 1959. Oil on canvas, 68¼ x 71½". Lent by Franklin Konigsberg, New York. Ill. p. 33

*Running White.* 1959. Oil on canvas, 7'4" x 68". Lent by Betty Parsons Gallery, New York

*Slip.* 1959. Oil on canvas, 60 x 50". Lent by Betty Parsons Gallery, New York. Ill. p. 30

*Summac.* 1959. Oil on canvas, 6'2" x 65". Lent by Betty Parsons Gallery, New York

*Wave Motif.* 1959. Oil on canvas, 60 x 7'10". Lent by Betty Parsons Gallery, New York. Ill. p. 31

*York.* 1959. Oil on canvas, 68 x 7'4". Lent by Betty Parsons Gallery, New York. Ill. p. 32

## ALFRED LESLIE

Born in New York, October 29, 1927. Grew up in New York. In U.S. Coast Guard, 1945–46. At New York University, 1948–49. First exhibited in *New Talent,* selected by Meyer Schapiro and Clement Greenberg, Kootz Gallery, New York, 1949. Lives in New York. One-man shows: Tibor de Nagy Gallery, New York, 1951, 1952, 1953, 1957; Robert Keene Gallery, Southampton, New York, 1957, 1958. International group exhibitions: IV International Art Exhibition of Japan, 1957; V Bienal, São Paulo, Brazil, 1959. In collections of Kunsthalle, Basel, Switzerland; Albright Art Gallery, Buffalo, New York; Whitney Museum of American Art, New York; Moderna Museet, Stockholm; University Art Gallery, University of Alabama.

*The Four-panel Green.* 1957. Oil on canvas, 12' x 11'4". Lent by Martha Jackson Gallery, New York. Ill. p. 37

*The Second Two-panel Horizontal.* 1958. Oil on canvas, 6' x 11'. Lent by Martha Jackson Gallery, New York. Ill. p. 36

"*Arrivato Zampano.*" 1959. Oil on canvas, 6'4" x 6'8". Lent by Martha Jackson Gallery, New York

*Baby's Curse.* 1959. Oil on canvas, 6' x 7'. Lent by Martha Jackson Gallery, New York. Ill. p. 35

"*Nix on Nixon.*" 1959. Oil on canvas, 6' x 6'7½". Lent by Martha Jackson Gallery, New York

## LANDÈS LEWITIN

Born in Cairo, Egypt, of Rumanian parentage, November 14, 1892. Studied in Egypt; at the Académies Libres, Paris; at the National Academy of Design and Art Students League, New York. Lived in France from about 1928 to 1939; has lived in New York since. First exhibited at Salon des Surindépendants, Paris, 1937. One-man shows in New York: Egan Gallery, 1947, 1949; Rose Fried Gallery, 1959; also Stable Gallery (with Joseph Cornell), 1955; Rose Fried Gallery (with Vicente and Yunkers), 1958.

*Forget It.* c.1954. Oil on canvas, 21 x 34". Lent by Rose Fried Gallery, New York. Ill. p. 38

*You Would Too.* c.1954. Oil and glass on canvas, 18 x 24". Lent by Rose Fried Gallery, New York

*22 Working Drawings.* c.1954. Colored ink and watercolor on paper, 3 x 5½" each. Lent by the artist. Ill. p. 93

*Only Now Counts.* 1955. Oil and glass on canvas, 18 x 24". Lent by Rose Fried Gallery, New York

*Easy.* 1955–58. Oil and plastic, 34 x 21". Lent by Royal S. Marks, New York. Ill. p. 41

*Knockout.* 1955–59. Oil and glass on canvas, 23⅞ x 17⅞". Lent by Rose Fried Gallery, New York. Ill. p. 39

*Think of Me, Dear.* c.1956. Oil and plastic, 23 x 11". Lent by Rose Fried Gallery, New York. Ill. p. 41

*And They Never Change (And Then There Were None).* 1957–58. Plastic emulsion on canvas, 40 x 60". Lent by Royal S. Marks, New York. Ill. p. 40

*Listen.* 1958. Oil on canvas, 44 x 30". Lent by Rose Fried Gallery, New York

## RICHARD LYTLE

Born in Albany, New York, February 14, 1935. Started attending painting classes at nine years of age. Studied at Cooper Union, New York, 1952–55; at Yale University, 1955–57, B.F.A. 1957. Teaching fellowship at Yale, 1956–58. Fulbright fellowship to Italy, 1958–59. In group shows at Kanegis Gallery, Boston, 1957, 1959; New Haven Art Festival, 1958; American Federation of Arts exhibition circulated in South America by U.S. Information Agency, 1956–59. Represented in collection of the Museum of Modern Art, New York. Lives in New Haven, Connecticut.

*Icarus Descended.* 1958. Oil on canvas, 62⅜ x 70¼". The Museum of Modern Art, New York, Elizabeth Bliss Parkinson Fund. Ill. p. 45

*Encounter.* 1959. Oil on canvas, 71" x 6'7". Lent by the artist

*The Oracle.* 1959. Oil on canvas, 6'7" x 9'10½". Lent by the artist

*The Possessed.* 1959. Oil on canvas, 8'2¾" x 6'7". Lent by the artist. Ill. p. 43

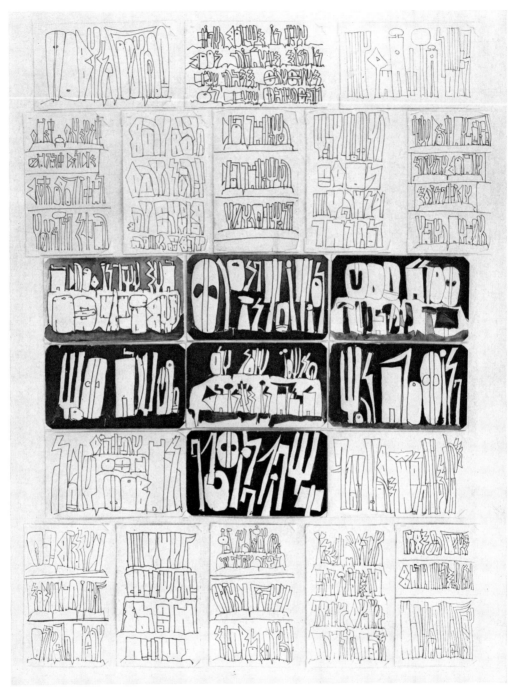

Landès Lewitin: 22 working drawings. c.1954. Colored ink and watercolor, 3 x 5½″ each.
Owned by the artist

*Prometheus.* 1959. Oil on canvas, 6'7" x 71". Lent by the artist. Ill. p. 44

*Verge.* 1959. Oil on canvas, 6'7" x 71". Lent by the artist. Ill. p. 46

*Loom.* 1959. Oil on canvas, 8' x 10'. Lent by the artist

## ROBERT MALLARY

Born in Toledo, Ohio, December 2, 1917. Grew up in Berkeley, California. Studied at Escuela de las Artes del Libro, Mexico City, 1938–39; Painters' Workshop School, Boston, 1941–42; Academia San Carlos, Mexico City, 1942–43. Associated with Orozco, 1943, in research project on experimental media. Taught at California School of Art, Los Angeles, 1949–50; Hollywood Art Center School, 1950–54; University of New Mexico, 1955–59; now teaching at Pratt Institute, Brooklyn, New York. Lives in New York. In many group exhibitions in Mexico and California, from 1939 on. One-man shows in California: San Francisco Museum of Art, 1944; Crocker Art Gallery, Sacramento, 1944, 1953; Third Street Gallery, Los Angeles, 1951; Santa Barbara Museum of Art, 1952; San Diego Fine Arts Society, 1952; Gump's, San Francisco, 1953. In New Mexico: University of New Mexico, 1956, 1957, 1958, 1959; Santa Fe Museum, 1958; Roswell Museum and Art Center, 1959. In New York: Urban Gallery, 1954. In collections of University of New Mexico, Albuquerque; Roswell Museum and Art Center, Roswell, New Mexico; Museum of Modern Art, New York.

*In Flight.* 1957. Wood, polyester resin, paint, sand on plywood, 43½" x 6'7⅝". The Museum of Modern Art, New York. Ill. p. 49

*Head of Bull.* 1958. Composition stone in resin base, 33 x 33". Lent by the artist. Ill. p. 50

*Lethe.* 1958. Composition stone in resin base, 54 x 6'5". Lent by the artist

*Nambe.* 1958. Composition stone in resin base, 6'5" x 49". Lent by Philip C. Johnson, New York. Ill. p. 51

*Sanctum.* 1958–59. Composition stone in resin base, 54½" x 6'1½". Lent by the artist

*Prison Yard.* 1959. Composition stone in resin base, 6'9½" x 57¾". Lent by the artist. Ill. p. 48

## LOUISE NEVELSON

Born in Kiev, Russia, 1900. Came to the United States in 1905; lived in Rockland, Maine. Studied with Kenneth Hayes Miller at Art Students League, New York, 1929–30; with Hans Hofmann in Munich, Germany, 1931. Archeological studies in Mexico and Central America. Lives in New York. One-man shows: Nierendorf Gallery, New York, 1940, 1943, 1946; Grand Central Moderns, New York, 1955, 1956, 1957, 1958; Galerie Jeanne Bucher, Paris, 1958 (with two other artists); Gres Gallery, Washington, D.C., 1958; Martha Jackson Gallery, New York, 1959. In collections of Birmingham Museum of Art, Birmingham, Alabama; Museum of Fine Arts of Houston, Texas; Newark Museum, Newark, New Jersey; Brooklyn Museum, Museum of Modern Art and Whitney Museum of American Art, New York; Carnegie Institute, Pittsburgh; Farnsworth Art Museum, Rockland, Maine; Brandeis University, Waltham, Mass.

*Dawn's Wedding Feast.* 1959. Wood wall constructions, columns, an arch, etc., painted white, filling a gallery 22 by 24' and 14' high. Made especially for this exhibition. Lent by Martha Jackson Gallery, N.Y. Ill. pp. 53–56

## ROBERT RAUSCHENBERG

Born in Port Arthur, Texas, 1925. In U.S. Navy. Studied at Kansas City Art Institute, at Académie Julian, Paris, 1947; with Josef Albers at Black Mountain College, North Carolina, 1948–49; with Vaclav Vytlacil and Morris Kantor at Art Student's League, New York, 1949–50. Resident artist at Black Mountain College, summer 1952. Traveled in Italy and North Africa, 1952–53. Has lived since then in New York. One-man shows: Stable Gallery, New York, 1953; Galleria del'Obelisco, Rome, 1953; Galleria d'Arte Contemporanea, Florence, 1953; Egan Gallery, New York, 1955; Leo Castelli, New York, 1958; Galleria La Tartaruga, Rome, 1959. In group shows since 1951, including international exhibitions: Carnegie International, Pittsburgh, 1958; Documenta II, Kassel, Germany, 1959; V Bienal, São Paulo, Brazil, 1959; Exposition International du Surréalisme, Paris, 1959–60; I Biennale, Paris, 1959. In collection of Albright Art Gallery, Buffalo, New York.

*Satellite.* 1955. Combine-painting with pheasant, 6'8" x 42½". Lent by Dr. and Mrs. Ernest Zeisler, Chicago. Ill. p. 61

*The Wager.* 1957-59. Combine-painting, 6'9" x 12'4" in 4 sections. Lent by Leo Castelli Gallery, New York

*\*Curfew.* 1958. Combine-painting, 57¼ x 39½". Lent by Mr. and Mrs. Donald H. Peters, New York. Ill. p. 62

*\*Double Feature.* 1959. Combine-painting, 7'7" x 52". Lent by Mr. and Mrs. Robert Scull, Great Neck, New York. Ill. p. 59

*Kickback.* 1959. Combine-painting, 6'3" x 32". Lent by Mr. and Mrs. William Rubin, New York

*\*The Magician.* 1959. Combine-painting, 65½ x 38½". Lent by Mrs. Leo Castelli, New York. Ill. p. 63

*\*Summer Storm.* 1959. Combine-painting, 6'7" x 63". Lent by Mr. and Mrs. Ira Haupt, New York. Ill. p. 60

## JULIUS SCHMIDT

Born in Stamford, Connecticut, June 2, 1923. Studied at Cranbrook Academy of Art, Bloomfield Hills, Michigan; B.F.A. 1952, M.F.A. 1955. In U.S. Navy, 1942-50. Traveled in Europe, 1953-54; studied with Ossip Zadkine in Paris and at the Academy of Fine Arts in Florence. Taught at Cranbrook Academy of Art, 1952-53; Silvermine Guild School of Art, New Canaan, Connecticut, summers 1953-54; Cleveland Institute of Art, summer 1957; Kansas City Art Institute, 1954-59; now teaching at Rhode Island School of Design, Providence. Lives in Providence. In many group shows since 1950. One-man show: William Rockhill Nelson Gallery of Art, Kansas City, Missouri, 1959. In collections of Art Institute of Chicago; William Rockhill Nelson Gallery of Art, Kansas City.

*Bronze sculpture.* 1957. Cast bronze, 23" high. Lent by Mr. and Mrs. Richard M. Hollander, Kansas City, Missouri

*\*Bronze sculpture.* 1957. Cast bronze, 23" high. Lent by James Baldwin, Mission, Kansas. Ill. p. 68

*\*Bronze sculpture.* 1958. Cast bronze, 23" long. Lent by Walter S. Goodhue, Alexandria, Virginia. Ill. p. 66

*\*Bronze sculpture.* 1958. Cast bronze, 24" high. Lent by Mr. and Mrs. Patrick J. Kelleher, Princeton, New Jersey. Ill. p. 68

*\*Iron sculpture.* 1958. Cast iron, 13" long. Lent by Rev. Robert C. Hunsicker, New York. Ill. p. 69

*\*Iron sculpture.* 1958. Cast iron relief, 14 x 31". Lent by the artist. Ill. p. 66

*Iron sculpture.* 1959. Cast iron, 15½" long. Lent by H. Marc Moyens, Alexandria, Virginia

*Iron sculpture.* 1959. Cast iron, 55" high. Lent by Dr. and Mrs. Justin L. Mooney, Mission, Kansas

*\*Iron sculpture.* 1959. Cast iron, copper-plated, 6' high. Lent by the artist. Ill. p. 67

## RICHARD STANKIEWICZ

Born in Philadelphia, Pennsylvania, October 18, 1922. Grew up in Detroit. In U.S. Navy, 1941-47: Alaska, Seattle, San Francisco, Hawaii. Studied at Hans Hofmann School of Fine Arts, New York, 1948-49; at Atelier Fernand Léger, Paris, 1950; at Atelier Ossip Zadkine, Paris, 1950-51. Lives in New York. In many group exhibitions in New York, Philadelphia, Chicago, Denver, Minneapolis, Houston, Los Angeles, Pittsburgh, etc. from 1953 on. One of three Americans in exhibition of young Italian and foreign artists, 29th Biennale, Venice, 1958. One-man shows: Hansa Gallery, New York, 1953 (two shows), 1954, 1956, 1957, 1958; Stable Gallery, New York, 1959. In collections of Albright Art Gallery, Buffalo, New York; Museum of Modern Art and Whitney Museum of American Art, New York.

*\*Committee.* 1954. Steel, 14" high. Lent by Horace Richter, Mt. Gilead, North Carolina. Ill. p. 71

*\*Panel.* 1955. Iron and steel, 68" x 11'9". Lent by Stable Gallery, New York. Ill. p. 74

*\*Urchin in the Grass.* 1956. Iron and steel, 23½" high. Lent by Philip C. Johnson, New York. Ill. p. 71

*\*Instruction.* 1957. Iron and steel, 12½" high. The Museum of Modern Art, New York, Philip C. Johnson Fund. Ill. p. 73

*\*Travels of the Pussycat King.* 1957. Iron and steel, 13" high. Lent by Richard Brown Baker, New York. Ill. p. 73

*Armillary.* 1958. Iron and steel, 46" high. Lent by Stable Gallery, New York

*\*Diving to the Bottom of the Ocean.* 1958. Iron and steel, 54½" high. Private collection, New York. Ill. p. 75

*\*Fish Lurking.* 1958. Iron and steel, 48¼" high. Lent by Mr. and Mrs. Albert H. Newman, Chicago. Ill. p. 72

*Untitled.* 1959. Iron and steel, 24½" high. Lent by Stable Gallery, New York

## FRANK STELLA

Born in Malden, Massachusetts, May 12, 1936. Lived in Malden and Melrose, Massachusetts. Studied painting at Phillips Academy, Andover, Massachusetts, with Patrick Morgan; with William Seitz and Stephen Greene at Princeton University, from which he graduated in 1958. Has painted in New York since. Exhibited with two other young American painters at Oberlin College, Oberlin, Ohio, 1959. In group shows at Tibor de Nagy Gallery and Leo Castelli Gallery, New York, 1959. Lives in New York.

*Arundel Castle. 1959. Oil on canvas, 10′11½″ x 6′1″. Lent by Leo Castelli Gallery, New York. Ill. p. 79

*"Die Fahne Hoch!" 1959. Oil on canvas, 10′11½″ x 6′1″. Lent by Leo Castelli Gallery, New York. Ill. p. 77

*The Marriage of Reason and Squalor. 1959. Oil on canvas, 7′6¾″ x 11′¾″. Lent by Leo Castelli Gallery, New York. Ill. p. 78

*Tomlinson Court Park. 1959. Oil on canvas, 7′1″ x 9′1¾″. Lent by Leo Castelli Gallery, New York. Ill. p. 78

## ALBERT URBAN

Born in Frankfurt am Main, Germany, July 22, 1909. Studied with Max Beckmann and Willi Baumeister in Frankfurt. Assistant teacher at Kunstschule, Frankfurt. Fellowships to study in Italy, France and Switzerland. To London, 1939; to U.S.A., 1940. Lived in New York until his death in April, 1959. One-man shows: Schneider Galleries, Frankfurt, Germany, 1928; Kunstverein, Frankfurt; Carlen Galleries, Philadelphia, 1941; Weyhe Gallery, New York, 1943, 1944; Kleemann Gallery, New York, 1946, 1947; Zabriskie Gallery, New York, 1958. In collections of the Addison Gallery of American Art, Andover, Massachusetts; Museum of Fine Arts, Boston; Brooklyn Museum, Metropolitan Museum of Art and Museum of Modern Art, New York; Seattle Art Museum, Seattle, Washington; National Gallery of Art, Washington, D.C.

Oedipus. 1958. Oil on canvas, 56 x 58″. Lent by Mrs. Albert Urban, New York

Painting. 1958. Oil on canvas, 68 x 71″. Lent by Mrs. Albert Urban, New York

Painting. 1959. Oil on canvas, 71 x 68″. Lent by Mrs. Albert Urban, New York

Painting. 1959. Oil on canvas, 71 x 68″. Lent by Mrs. Albert Urban, New York

*Painting. 1959. Oil on canvas, 68 x 70″. Lent by Mrs. Albert Urban, New York. Ill. p. 81

*Painting. 1959. Oil on canvas, 54 x 56″. Lent by Mrs. Albert Urban, New York. Ill. p. 82

*Painting. 1959. Oil on canvas, 72 x 68″. The Museum of Modern Art, New York. Ill. p. 83

## JACK YOUNGERMAN

Born in Louisville, Kentucky, March 25, 1926. At University of North Carolina, U.S. Navy training program, 1944–46. University of Missouri, B.A. degree, 1947. Lived in Paris, 1947–56. Studied at Ecole des Beaux-Arts. First exhibited in group shows in Paris at Galerie Maeght, 1950; Galerie Denise René, 1952. Traveled in Europe and the Near East, 1952–56; worked on architectural projects in Lebanon and Iraq with the architect Michel Ecochard. Designed Histoire de Vasco by Georges Schehade for Jean-Louis Barrault, Paris, 1956. To New York to live, December 1956. Designed Deathwatch by Jean Genet, New York, 1958. One-man shows: Galerie Arnaud, Paris, 1951; Betty Parsons Gallery, New York, 1958; also Gres Gallery, Washington, D.C. (with Edgar Negret), 1957; Kimura Gallery, Tokyo (with Motherwell, Newman, Okada, Rothko, Tobey), 1959; Carnegie International, Pittsburgh; Corcoran Biennial, Washington, D.C., etc. In collections of the Museum of Modern Art, New York; Chase Manhattan Bank, New York; Reynolds Metals Building, Richmond, Virginia.

*Aquitaine. 1959. Oil on canvas, 70 x 49½″. The Museum of Modern Art, New York, Larry Aldrich Foundation Fund. Ill. p. 85

*Aztec III. 1959. Oil on canvas, 6′3″ x 7′1″. Private collection, New York. Ill. p. 88

*Big Black. 1959. Oil on canvas, 7′7″ x 70″. Lent by Betty Parsons Gallery, New York. Ill. p. 87

*Coenties Slip. 1959. Oil on canvas, 6′9″ x 63″. Lent by Betty Parsons Gallery, New York. Ill. p. 89

Palmyra. 1959. Oil on canvas, 70¼ x 55⅛″. Lent by Betty Parsons Gallery, New York

*Ram. 1959. Oil on canvas, 7′6″ x 63½″. Lent by Betty Parsons Gallery, New York. Ill. p. 86

Talmont. 1959. Oil on canvas, 65 x 65″. Lent by Betty Parsons Gallery, New York